HISTORY IN CAM~~ERA~~

WEST COAST SHIPPING

M. K. STAMMERS

SHIRE PUBLICATIONS LTD

2

Printed in Great Britain by C. I. Thomas & Sons (Haverfordwest) Ltd, Press Buildings, Merlins Bridge, Haverfordwest.

The cover photograph is of the Isle of Man steamer off Liverpool Landing Stage in 1972. The photograph on the title page shows a typical steam coaster, the 'Afon Morlais', owned by William Coombs & Sons of Llanelli until sold to John S. Monks of Liverpool in 1956. Below: The river Mersey off Liverpool Landing Stage about 1890.

Contents

Introduction 5

Ports of the west coast 13

Sailing ships 15

Steamships 27

Fishing 39

Safe navigation and lifesaving 45

Bibliography 86

Photographic acknowledgements 86

Index 87

1. *A Mersey flat, on a broad reach with the wind and tide in her favour, surges on down river to pick up a cargo in Liverpool docks. Unlike other similar coastal barges flats carried no leeboards; they relied on their fine entry and run aft and small keel to prevent them from going too much to leeward. Flatmen were masters at manoeuvring their craft. With no rails and a tackle on the forestay for lowering the mast she is an up-river or 'inside' flat.*

Introduction

This book is a photographic survey of the ships, seamen and ports of the west coast of England and Wales from the mid nineteenth century to the mid twentieth century, which was a period of extraordinary maritime activity along this stretch of coastline. In the mid nineteenth century the small ports could generate sufficient capital and expertise to build, own and run fleets of small sailing ships. Many coastal settlements looked to the sea for transport of their exports and their imports, particularly coal, and their inhabitants earned an often precarious livelihood from fishing and seafaring. It was a period before the roads and railways could offer a competitive land service. It was also a period of rapid industrial expansion when coal and iron were staple cargoes and indeed whole ports such as those of Cumbria and South Wales were almost entirely devoted to their handling and shipment to all parts of the world. This was also an era which saw the spread of an elaborate network of steam services for cargo and passengers to and from the major ports, especially Liverpool, across the Atlantic and to many other parts of the world. There was a parallel development of steamer services to Ireland, the Isle of Man and along the coast. Railways made it possible for large numbers of working people from the industrial towns inland to travel to the newly established seaside resorts, perhaps to indulge in a trip on a paddle steamer or a tea of freshly boiled shrimps caught by the local inshore fishing fleet. In all the ports there were skilled craftsmen building and repairing ships and boats in wood, iron or steel that ranged from the fast, weatherly and beautiful schooners of Portmadoc to prefabricated stern-wheel paddle steamers built at Northwich for export to distant rivers of Africa.

Destitution, injury and death were constant threats in the ordinary mariner's life, as well as an infinite amount of backbreaking toil. Yet in many ways there was much satisfaction in the work and indeed there were still opportunities for the able and thrifty to move from working to owning small coasting vessels. They were on the whole fine seamen, capable of manoeuvring their craft with great skill and precision, with an inherited fund of knowledge of these coastal waters, of tides, rocks, sandbanks, shoals and weather lore, and with no more than a few basic pieces of navigational equipment. But the lee shore and the treacherous gales of the Irish Sea were constant hazards. Wrecks were all too common. Not every vessel was well maintained and some only stayed afloat by constant heartbreaking pumping and a quick bit of caulking at low tide. The lifeboats performed many brave rescues and some of the first lifeboat stations, such as those built by the Liverpool Corporation in the 1800s, were established on the west coast, and the setting up of a National Lifeboat Service was inspired by Sir William Hilary as a result of his experiences of wrecks on the Isle of Man.

We have moved on: the coal and iron ports are no longer booming; deep-water sailing ships that carried so much of the coal before 1914 have vanished; passenger liners no longer call at Liverpool; the paddle steamers have all gone and the few remaining excursion steamers are faced with a struggle against ever rising operating costs. Inshore fishing is not what it was; the shrimps no longer run thick off Southport and the nobbies, now all motorised, get fewer every year. The once great fishing port of Milford Haven no longer owns any trawlers. The cross-channel shipping services are in competition with aircraft. Pembroke Dock is no longer a naval base, but an industrial estate. Bristol docks are due to close. Liverpool has closed its South docks. Amlwch, no longer exporting copper, is the service base for a deep-water oil terminal. Virtually every aspect of our west coast shipping has changed. So we are looking back to a recent era in our maritime history which has disappeared but for a few remnants. Its history is preserved in documents, a few surviving vessels like the *Great Britain* or the schooner *Kathleen and May,* built at Connah's Quay, old harbours and hulks rebuilt and rerigged in the imagination of the enthusiast, such as the trows on the Severn's shore, the models in museums, the memories of old seafarers, and photographs.

Ship photography started with Fox Talbot's famous picture of the *Great Britain* fitting out at Cumberland Basin, Bristol, in 1844. It was apt that the image of this forerunner of all modern screw steamships should be caught and made permanent by the new technique of photography. The photograph is too well known to warrant publication again. (Readers will find it in Rear Admiral Brock and Basil Greenhill's *Sail and steam in Britain and America,* page 74, for example.) From the 1840s the spread of photographic knowledge and the improvement of its methods was rapid.

IG DILIGENCE *of* **BARMOUTH OWEN EDWARDS COMMANDER**

2. This primitive watercolour of the 'Diligence' emphasises the chunky box-like shape of this early nineteenth-century craft. Her rigging has been accurately pencilled in with a ruler. A trysail mast is shown abaft the main mast. Technically this makes her a snow, not a brig. Two-masted square-rigged vessels like the 'Diligence' were superseded by the more economical and efficient topsail schooners. The 'Diligence' was built on the Mawddach in 1816. She was only 98 tons. In October 1848 she was lost on the Kentish Knock while on passage from Portmadoc to Newcastle. She is a reminder of the once flourishing port of Barmouth and its shipbuilding industry, which lost out to its new rivals, Portmadoc and the railway, in the 1860s. Watercolours or oil portraits of ships were frequently commissioned by proud captains and owners from pier-head artists, often at a cost of a few shillings. Until recently, such paintings were to be seen in the homes of retired seafarers and their descendants in the little ports of North Wales.

This is not the book in which to go into the technical problems; but the work of men like the Reverend Calvert Jones of Swansea provides the maritime historian with excellent pictorial evidence of types of vessels that have long disappeared — types otherwise known only through written evidence or oil paintings and prints where the rendering of detail is naturally often subject to artistic rather than technical considerations. Much of the early photographers' work has not survived; little or nothing

3. *Swansea harbour in the 1840s. This remarkable photograph by the Rev. Calvert Jones shows the type of wooden sailing ships that carried Britain's expanding trade in the eighteenth and early nineteenth centuries: deep, bluff-bowed, flat-floored vessels sitting on the mud of the then tidal harbour. Most of them were probably engaged in the Swansea copper-ore trade. But for the paddle tug, the scene could have been one of fifty years earlier.*

beyond carte-de-visite portraits exists of the professional photographers' work in Liverpool of the 1850s and 1860s. Samuel Walters, the best of the Liverpool marine artists, photographed ships in the Mersey and none of his prints are known to exist. The case of the Liverpool photographer who tipped his old glass negatives into the foundation trenches of his new house is unfortunately not unique. The cumbersome equipment of the almost standard wet-collodion negatives, while producing excellent results, may have inhibited the spread of photographing ships as a pastime. When the dry-plate negative became generally available in the late 1880s, there seems to have been an explosion in the number of photographs taken by amateur enthusiasts bent on recording the ships and not just producing a pleasing image. The father of the late Ernest Worthy took a remarkable series of the Mersey ferries and the schooners sailing up the Mersey at this period. His photograph of the brigantine *Brothers* of Arklow is included in this present selection. Large numbers of photographs were also taken for business or legal purposes; the Mersey Docks and Harbour Board had its own photographic department whose excellent glass negatives have now been deposited with the Merseyside Maritime Museum. Many of their photographs recorded the progress of construction work on new docks and these often show interesting vessels like the old flat *Chester* which were quite incidental to the purpose of taking the photograph.

This survey draws on many different sources, and such is the amazing number of photographs available that I have had to limit my selection. The west coast of England and Wales from the Scottish border has so many ports and harbours that it is not possible to illustrate every one. Within these hundred or so illustrations I have tried to pick out a

4. Swansea pilot schooners, 1845. These vessels retained the old seventeenth and eighteenth-century schooner rig to meet the special conditions of working out of Swansea harbour. The pole-masted rig with a running bowsprit was handy for sailing in the crowded anchorage and beating out to sea against the prevailing south-west winds. This rig was also found on the Aberystwyth beachboats and the fishing wherries of Allonby, Cumbria, in the nineteenth century.

5. *In 1858, George's Dock, Liverpool, was packed with small brigs and schooners. This was the centre of Liverpool's fresh-fruit trade. The forest of masts stretches into the distance to the northern docks. Deep-water traffic was still carried in small sailing ships and as many as fifty vessels might enter the Mersey on one tide. George's Dock has now been filled by the dock board, and the Cunard offices and the Goree Piazza warehouses have been replaced by a car park.*

representative selection and I have also tried to complement the many excellent picture history books on shipping that have already been published. Thus I have drawn my southern boundary at the Devon coast because I feel that the schooners and fishing craft of the South-west have been dealt with so authoritatively and in such detail that there is little point in covering the same ground again. This does not mean that these vessels are entirely excluded; there is an excellent picture of the barquentine *May Cory*, built at Bideford, on the grid-iron at Bristol. I have also tried to focus attention on ships and ports that I feel have been neglected. Incredibly, this includes Liverpool, the second port of the kingdom. An emphasis on Liverpool also illustrates the flow of trade between this large port and the many smaller ports of the west coast. The order of illustrations is largely chronological, but certain themes run strongly throughout: for example, the many different types of coastal sailing craft — schooners, flats, trows, pilot boats, etc — and all the service vessels so essential to the safety and maintenance of a port — lightships, dredgers, tugs, coal barges, etc. The more 'glamorous' deep-sea passenger liners and naval vessels certainly appear but usually in connection with the work of some type of small service craft such as tugs. The essential human element is not omitted nor is the once important shipbuilding industry. Many of the photographs speak for themselves; it is hoped that the captions and the general introduction on some of the main types of shipping illustrated will enhance and inform the reader's enjoyment of the photographs.

6. A busy scene at the entrance to the Mersey about 1865. The paddle ferry 'Gem' steams away from the newly erected landing stage at New Brighton with a full load of passengers bound for Liverpool. In the background a topsail schooner and a full-rigged ship towed by a tug are making their way up river.

7. *Although boiler pressures were kept deliberately low in the first paddle steamers, boilers occasionally burst through bad construction or mismanagement. The results were usually devastating. In November 1866 the Cardiff tug 'Black Eagle No. 1' blew up while towing a Norwegian barque up the river Avon, leaving very little of her stern section intact.*

8. *A topsail schooner makes the most of a favouring wind to carry her down the Mersey from the Sloyne anchorage. Note that one of her anchors has not been stowed. Every sail is set except her fore staysail. She has an old-fashioned look — with her boxy hull, long jib-boom, deep narrow fore topsails and jackyard main topsail. It is a pity that she cannot be identified.*

Ports of the west coast

Ships need a landing place or port for loading and unloading their cargoes. The west coast has many ports. Some have grown very large and cater for ocean-going vessels; others were no more than a creek or inlet where the occasional coaster landed her cargo. Their history goes back to Roman times at least: for example, archaeologists have excavated a Roman port on the Dee near Chester. The charters and customs rolls of our medieval kings tell of growing trade with Ireland and the Continent and a recognition of ports as specific points for the two-way exchange of traffic between land and water. New ports such as Liverpool or Milford were recognised by royal charter and prosperous ports such as Bristol or Chester were taxed by the king's customs officers on their imports and exports. But the volume of trade remained quite small until the expansion of maritime commerce at the time of the industrial revolution. Traffic was mainly coastal and Irish until the development of English overseas trade at the beginning of the eighteenth century. Bristol, Liverpool, Lancaster and Whitehaven all took some part in this, especially in the trade to the West Indies and North America. The first enclosed docks were built at this time. They ensured the safety of larger deep-sea ships and improved their 'turnround times'.

While the deep-sea ships carried British goods to an expanding overseas market, coastal shipping was a cheap method of moving all the bulky low-cost raw materials such as coal, iron ore and china clay, so vital to Britain's rapidly growing industries. The improvement of river navigations, followed by the digging of a network of canals, extended this cheap water carriage from the ports to inland towns. Liverpool by 1820 was connected by water to the booming textile towns of Lancashire and Yorkshire, the Staffordshire potteries and the Black Country round Birmingham; Newport, Swansea and Cardiff all increased their coal exports when linked by canal to the mines in the valleys to their north.

Existing ports were extended and new ports created. Swansea's tidal harbour, as photographed by the Reverend Calvert Jones in the 1840s, was transformed into deep-water enclosed docks. The new technology of steam power was employed to build and work larger and larger docks. By the 1840s steam cranes, dredgers, tugs, hydraulic pumping engines and railway locomotives enabled the ports to handle more traffic than ever before. The new railways provided a faster and ultimately cheaper service for the inland industrial towns. The railway companies also built their own new ports as outlets for their passenger and freight traffic. Thus the larger ports of the west coast grew into very complex organisations with all kinds of machinery and storage such as coal hoists, conveyors, refrigerated warehouses, floating landing stages, etc. This process has continued with such modern innovations as containers and roll-on roll-off berths. But we must not forget that these nineteenth-century ports also employed thousands of low-paid casual dock labourers to sling, winch, manhandle, shovel and barrow the cargoes of the ships in dock.

The smaller ports throve too. Along the Cumbrian coast Harrington, Maryport, Workington, Whitehaven and Millom all had their harbours enlarged in the nineteenth century. This was for the huge quantities of coal and iron which they shipped both coastwise and overseas. Elsewhere, in Wales for example, it was much the same story. The tremendous rise in demand for building materials brought about the construction of new harbours such as Portmadoc for slate and Connah's Quay for bricks and tiles, and further south in Dyfed Tenby and Saundersfoot dispatched thousands of tons of best anthracite from the local collieries. Many of these ports are now in decay. The demand for coal has slackened and many coastal pits have closed; the rich iron-ore deposits of Cumbria and the copper of Anglesey have been exhausted. The end of sailing ships and the increasing size of powered vessels has cut off some of the smallest ports, while others like Aberystwyth lost their battle to keep their harbour from silting up. The big ports have closed and filled obsolete docks. The railways and later the motor lorry have deprived the coastal ships of much of their cargoes and what trade that remains is often carried on by foreign vessels. The reasons for the change and decline of these ports in the twentieth century are very complex and vary from port to port. I have suggested just a few. But the photographs provide us with a vital record of what these ports were like when they were still busy and alive with ships.

Sailing ships

These photographs show what large numbers of sailing ships there once were in the west coast ports. They also show the amazing diversity of build and rig. First there were the ocean-going carriers: they tended to be full-rigged ships or barques. In the 1840s they were still on average quite small, perhaps about 500 tons, and rather bluff in the bows. By the 1850s their hull design changed radically to produce a much larger, faster type of ship to work in new trades such as the emigrant trade to Australia and the China tea trade. Many of the vessels were American-built. Rapid improvements in the economy of steam propulsion brought an end to these premier trades and for the rest of the time that deep-sea sailing ships were built they were increasingly constructed of iron and steel and designed to carry the maximum amount of cargo at minimum cost. The barque rig was often substituted for the traditional square sails on the sail plan of all masts because it saved on maintenance and the number of the crew without much loss of speed. Towards the end of the nineteenth century the sailing-ship business tended to be reduced to certain bulk carrying trades because of the increasing competition from steamships. One of the most important of these was the carriage of coal from the ports of South Wales and, for the return voyage, grain from San Francisco or Australia. These large sailing vessels were to be seen in significant if declining numbers up to the First World War in many west coast ports. Silloth, for example, received its last grain consignment by sail in the Norwegian ship *Lota* in 1914. Many were lost as a result of war action and after a short boom in 1919-20 the world economic situation made them no longer viable except for a few Scandinavian-owned ships in the Australian grain trade.

The coastal cargoes were carried by many, many small wooden vessels — brigs, snows, brigantines, topsail schooners (two- and three-masted), ketches, sloops, flats and trows. They were owned and built all along the

A WHITEHAVEN SHIPYARD

9. *The craft of wooden shipbuilding was practised in many west coast ports. But by the 1860s the production of wooden deep-sea vessels was declining in favour of iron ones. This view shows one of the last big wooden full-rigged ships to be built at T. & J. Brocklebank's yard at Whitehaven. She is the 'Tenasserim', launched in 1861 for Brocklebanks' Calcutta trade.*

coastline. The traditional division of ownership into sixty-four shares ensured a wide dispersion of investors among the mariners, merchants and tradesmen of the coastal towns and villages. Some places owned vessels in surprising numbers: in 1865, for instance, the Ship Registers of Caernarvon listed over four hundred locally owned vessels. This included the expanding fleet of schooners based on Portmadoc. Other important coastal ship-owning centres included Bridgwater, Aberystwyth, Connah's Quay, Runcorn and Barrow. Many of their vessels sailed in deep-water trades as well, for example in the fruit trade to Liverpool and Bristol from the Mediterranean or in the copper-ore trade from South America to Swansea. The finest of these small ocean-going traders were probably the brigs and schooners of Portmadoc which from 1879 specialised in the salt-cod trade from Newfoundland to the Mediterranean. This difficult voyage was often undertaken in the stormy months of autumn and winter. Some fine, fast schooners were built especially for this trade. But by the 1870s the general tendency was for the small ships to move out of the deep-sea trade into the home trades and for the fore and aft rigs — the ketch and

10. *A Liverpool shipwright with his guild's standard in the trades procession for Queen Victoria's visit in May 1886. It contains a selection of replicas of the tools of the craft including an adze, a broad axe, a hand saw, a caulking mallet and caulking irons, capped by a model ship in full sail. This splendid assembly is now in the Merseyside Maritime Museum's collection.*

11. Bristol about 1870: a view from Redcliff Parade across to the busy dockside. Casks and bundles lie on the open quay awaiting transport, and beyond there is an interesting jumble of buildings, all different but all serving the port, from the Bristol and Newport Screw Steam Packet Co's depot, to the Sailors' Home, two pubs, the Grove Tavern and the Coach and Horses, to the Cooper's workshop. The wooden three-masted barque in the centre is the West Indian trader 'Maria'. She is probably discharging a cargo of sugar and she is a reminder of Bristol's long association with the West Indies which went back to the slave-trading years of the eighteenth century.

the schooner — to displace the square-riggers. Back at the end of the eighteenth-century there were few cargo-carrying schooners, though there were many small open-deck schooners like the *Peggy* of 1791 which is preserved at Castletown Maritime Museum, Isle of Man. But from about the 1820s the topsail schooner became increasingly popular and ultimately the predominant rig of the small cargo carriers. The rig offered a neat compromise between fore and aft and square rigs which made it more adaptable and economical than the square-sailed brigs and snows. The available evidence suggests that it was first developed in the United States, possibly by adapting the brigantine by substituting a large gaff foresail for three staysails. But there were many variations: the old stone carrier *Oak*, built in 1836, carried so many square sails on her foremast that she looked like a brigantine. However, she also carried a gaff foresail and was registered as a schooner. Many vessels changed their rig according to their trading circumstances. Many lofty schooners finished up pole-masted or as ketches. The driving power of the square topsails was often replaced by a diesel engine in their last years. Hull designs varied from builder to builder. Few measured more than about 200 gross tons. The ships designed for ocean sailing tended to be a complex shape with hollow entrance, very few flat floors amidships and a good run aft, deep of draught and a lot of sheer. Others, especially those from the north-west ports such as Connah's Quay or Barrow, were intended principally for the coasting trade and tended to be shallower with flat floors and the rudder hung outboard. They could take ground at low tide easily and stay

12. *Sailing-ship owners took an interest in their ships beyond their trading accounts. Many went to inspect their ships whenever they were in a British port. Thomas Brocklebank (extreme right) and his marine superintendent, Captain Ray, are looking over his new ship 'Bolan' at Birkenhead in 1883. The other gentlemen are presumably the master and the two mates in shore-going dress. Brocklebank's were an old firm which originally started in Whitehaven in the eighteenth century. They did not buy their first steamship until 1891.*

13. *Liverpool pilot schooner 'Guide', No. 9, in the Mersey about 1880. The 'Guide' was launched in 1862 at Ramsey, Isle of Man, to replace the old cutter-rigged No. 9 boat, 'Liver'. 'The Pioneer', No. 6, introduced the schooner rig to the Liverpool service in 1852 when the ever increasing number of ships entering the Mersey made bigger pilot boats a necessity. The larger type of pilot boat, 67 tons, compared to the 41 tons of the existing cutters, would have been very difficult to handle if cutter-rigged. The 'Guide' was run down and sunk by T. & J. Harrison's steam 'Mariner' about two miles west-north-west of the Bar lightship on 25th February 1882.*

upright; they had a good cargo capacity and their ability to go about quickly meant they could often dispense with tugs. The Ashburners of Barrow probably produced the best compromise design between the two types.

The ketch rig came into favour about the same time as the schooner. Many later skippers considered it a handier rig than the schooner. It certainly tended to replace the single-masted rig for small craft. The sloops, cutters or smacks as they were variously known were often of no more than 40 or 50 tons gross and were capable of delivering to the most remote creeks and beaches. Many of them still carried the old eighteenth-century square sail for fair winds.

There were also two important types of sailing barge: the Severn trow and the Mersey flat. The trow, whose name is derived from the Anglo-

14. *Whitehaven harbour at low tide, about 1875. This was one of the oldest and most important ports of the north-west coast. Based on the coal and iron trade, at one time in the early eighteenth century Whitehaven rivalled Liverpool for numbers of ships. Note the contrast in sterns between the old brigantine 'Jane and Jessie' built in 1839 with stern windows, a schooner with a plain counter, and the great iron bulk-carrying three-masted ship at the opposite quay. She was undoubtedly the latest product of the famous Whitehaven Shipbuilding Co.*

Saxon for a drinking vessel or hollow trough, was originally a double-ended open-decked barge with a single square sail, working on the upper reaches of the Severn. By the eighteenth century there was a transom stern version, and this type, though still with an open hold, traded down the lower reaches of the river and into the estuary. Between about 1840 and 1860 trows underwent more changes and were converted to ketch or sloop rig. Small dumb lighters on the Avon which were similar to trows retained the square sail for use in favourable winds. Quite a few trows survived into the twentieth century, mainly in the coal trade, but few remained under sail by the 1920s. Many were towed as lighters and quite a number were well over hundred years old before they were discarded. It is fortunate that one trow has been preserved: the *Spry* of 1984 at the Ironbridge Gorge Museum.

The Mersey flats underwent a similar development with a change from square to sloop-rig in the mid eighteenth century and a gradual extension

15. *A very ancient coastal paddle steamer, 'Taff', complete with clipper bow and gingerbread round her stern, lying aground off the new Portishead dock, still being built in 1875. She was launched by Stotherts of Bristol in 1856 and from 1868 she was run by the Cardiff and Portishead Steamship Co. In summer she operated excursions to Ilfracombe and Tenby and in winter she sailed only as far as Newport and Cardiff.*

of their range from the Mersey and its tributaries to coastal work. The flat's hull was massively built with a flat bottom, rounded bilge, and a neat but short entry and run aft. A huge rudder was hung outboard on the sternpost. The sailing gear was very substantial with chain and wire rigging, and the mainsail had a characteristically high peak. The sails were tanned a splendid red with oak bark and seal oil. Most carried neither a topmast nor a bowsprit, but as flats increased in size a number were ketch-rigged. These ketch-rigged or 'jigger' flats were fitted with auxiliary engines and continued to work from the North Wales quarries and mines into the Mersey until the Second World War.

The pattern of trading for most coastal craft was of tramping — of picking up cargoes where they were offered. Some had a steady job for years like the ketch *Progress* which did nineteen continuous years in the Newfoundland trade and never came home. Many worked from the West Country ports with china clay to Runcorn, Ellesmere Port or Weston Point

16. *Docks at Avonmouth and Portishead were built at the mouth of the Avon to cope with the increasing tonnage of ships calling at the port of Bristol, and tucked away in the corner of the first Avonmouth dock lies the Scandinavian barque 'Vasco da Gama' (built 1875, 615 tons). She was just one of a fleet of small barques, brigs and schooners that brought cargoes of timber to England. Some survived in the trade till the 1930s. Note the typical windmill pump amidships. The lighter alongside the 'Vasco' appears to be the gutted hull of an old sailing ship — a common fate.*

17. *Portmadoc was developed as a new slate-exporting port in the 1820s. It prospered and built up a considerable fleet of small barques and brigs trading all over the world. In the late nineteenth century the port's famous topsail schooners were considered to be the finest of all the different British schooners. They dominated the trade with Newfoundland. Sailing ships were still being built and owned at Portmadoc till the First World War. This general view shows the port in the 1890s, crowded with ships loading slate. In the foreground there is a three-masted barque and three schooners; two more are being built at Morris's yard adjacent to the slate storage yard.*

and returned with coal cargoes. Passages could be long, and there could be long waits between cargoes when no money came in. Expenses could be heavy: there were bills for maintenance — sails and rigging were always expensive — and towage could be a costly item, plus harbour dues, food, wages, etc. It was a business that needed the utmost economy to make small dividends. An example of the random pattern of voyages are those of the *James Postlethwaite* of Barrow in 1884-5. She made twenty-six voyages in the year. Her voyages included Fleetwood to Plymouth, Plymouth to the Thames, the Medway to Eriska, Eriska to Ayr, Ayr to Newport (Gwent), Newport to Dundalk, and Dundalk to Whitehaven. Her cargoes included coal, bricks, cement, pig iron, timber and manure. Her best-paying freight was stone from Whitehaven to the Regents Canal at 7s 6d per ton and her worst coal from Connah's Quay to Barrow at 1s

18. *Discharging cargo by dolly winch at Canning Dock, Liverpool, about 1898. This time-honoured method of discharging cargo lingered in the coastal trade under sail where only small quantities were involved and a fast turnround time was not crucial. By the time of this photograph, most ocean-going sailing ships were fitted with an auxiliary boiler and steam winches. A gin block has been rigged from a temporary derrick on the schooner's foremast. Two men work the handles of the ship's dolly winch to lift the sacks clear of the hold while a third heaves on a line to swing the sacks on to the team wagon. The carter is busy with his sack barrow stowing the sacks. The men are probably dockers, but in smaller ports it was usual for the crew to carry out the loading and discharging of their own ship.*

19. *The smack-rigged 'Industry' of only 38 tons reminds us of the very small size of many coasting vessels and how they provided an essential and economical delivery service for many small coastal and river villages remote from the railway. The 'Industry' was built in 1871 and registered at the river Wye port of Chepstow. She was owned at Lydney and doubtless sailed from there with coal cargoes.*

20. *These trading smacks of 1870 lie at their moorings beneath the walls of Caernarvon Castle much like their medieval predecessors. They carried anything and everything along the coasts of North Wales and Cardigan Bay and quite a few sailed further afield to Spain and to the Mediterranean.*

10½d per ton, which were both little enough recompense. *James Postlethwaite* and quite a number of other schooners and ketches continued trading, usually with auxiliary engines, into the 1930s. A few survived the Second World War and carried on into the 1950s. Today at least three have been preserved: the *Result* at the Ulster Folk Museum; the *Kathleen and May* at London; and the *De Wadden* at Liverpool.

Steamships

The west coast ports were some of the first to use steamships, and engineers at Bristol and Liverpool especially played an important part in their early development. The first steamship on the west coast was probably a certain Mr Smith's seven-oared paddle steamer that was tried out on the Sankey Canal near Liverpool in 1793. In the following decade a number of other experimental boats were tried on neighbouring canals and there was also said to be a steamboat plying between Bristol and Bath by 1814. 1815 saw the first steamer in commercial service — the *Elizabeth*, built on the Clyde and plying between Liverpool and Runcorn. This year also saw the epic voyage of the *Thames* from the Clyde to London. She passed close to the Welsh shore at St Davids and called at Milford Haven, where she created much interest and demonstrated the power of steam by convincingly beating one of the locally based naval sloops in a race. Within the next five years regular steamship services were started from Holyhead to Dublin and from Liverpool to the Isle of Man, Belfast and Glasgow.

All the early steamers were fitted with side lever engines and low-pressure boilers that consumed huge quantities of coal. Deep-sea voyages were scarcely economic because of the amount of fuel that had to be carried. But in 1837 Brunel completed his *Great Western* paddle steamer which began the first regular steamship link across the Atlantic from Bristol to New York. There was also a number of rival companies based on Liverpool, but the most significant was the line started by Samuel Cunard in 1840 which had a government subsidy for carrying mails. This company prospered and became the famous Cunard Line. The 1840s saw important technical advances. These were nearly all incorporated in Brunel's second steamer, the *Great Britain*. She was completed at Bristol (where she is now preserved) in 1844 and was built of iron instead of wood and had a screw propeller instead of paddles. She set the pattern for all later steamships.

21. *Workington's new lifeboat, 'The Dodo', and her crew ready for action in 1886. Rowing lifeboats were stationed at many points along the west coast, and through the courage and tenacity of their crews many lives were saved. 'The Dodo' was given to Workington in 1886. She was a 34-foot self-righting boat with a crew of thirteen, and in her eleven launches she saved seventeen lives. She was condemned in 1899 and replaced by a similar boat of the same name.*

However, the problem of fuel economy was not cracked until some twenty years later. It was solved by the development of high-pressure boilers and compound engines that used the same steam twice instead of once. In the 1880s compound engines were extended to become triple-expansion engines and later quadruple-expansion engines. The Liverpool engineer and shipowner Alfred Holt played an important role in getting the compound engine established as a commercial proposition by profitably sending compound-engined steamers of his own design out to China in competition with the tea clippers from 1866 onwards. Sailing ships had dominated the long-distance trades until this time, but the new compound engines, the establishment of a worldwide network of coaling stations and the opening of the Suez Canal gave winning advantages to the steamer. Sailing ships still dominated in terms of numbers and many continued to be launched well into the 1890s, but they were increasingly confined to bulk carrying trades. Steamers grew in size and power, especially on the transatlantic routes where there was great competition between the steamship lines such as Cunard, Inman and White Star to provide the fastest, most luxurious passenger service.

22. Manx 'nickies' at Port St Mary, 1884. This type of fishing boat was used for drift-net fishing and was copied from the west Cornish luggers. They were fine sea boats and regularly made the passage round the north of Scotland to the Shetland fishery. Port St Mary was the second fishing port of the Isle of Man after Peel and as many as 125 boats were registered there in the 1880s. The boats in the foreground from left to right are CT50 'Leek', CT67 'Bessie', CT15 'Scotch Annie' and CT46 'Egret'. The shipwrights were hard at work on the 'Egret' fitting a new deck and bulwarks.

23. All the first steam trawlers were converted from paddle tugs, and in this view the Cardiff tug 'Her Majesty', built in 1877 and registered as CF70, is towing a group of sailing trawlers out of Milford Haven dock in the early 1890s. The leading boat is a Hull-registered vessel. Trawlers from all the main fishing ports, but particularly from Brixham, came to Milford and Tenby for a fishing season that lasted from June to September.

24. *When steam trawlers began to go fishing for weeks at a time ice became essential to preserve the catch. Milford Haven and other fishing ports imported ice from Scandinavia before local ice-making factories were built. This view shows a cargo of Norwegian ice being skated into the ice store at Milford in the 1890s.*

25. *The little 118-ton 'Welsh Prince' is cluttered like a Greek island steamer, with deckhouses, lifeboats, deck cargo and passengers. There does not seem to be space left for the puncheon-size casks they are loading. The staysails must have been necessary for steadying her with all that weight on deck. A little more water and she will leave Newport for Bristol. Until the opening of the Severn railway tunnel in 1886, she was one of the main links between South Wales and Bristol.*

26. *Castletown harbour, Isle of Man, 1884: a scene of thriving maritime activity with coastal schooners at the quays and a nobby, CT51 'Faith', and a nicky, CT42 'Ceres', in the foreground. Their characteristic hull shape copied from the Cornish luggers is clearly to be seen. The difference between a nobby and a nicky was mainly one of rig, although even the experts have had difficulty in laying down a precise distinction. The nicky, which came first, had a simple lug rig, while the nobby was an improvement devised in the 1880s with a raked mainmast to accommodate a foresail and a sliding bowsprit for a jib. Both types were about 34 tons and measured about 50 feet long by 12 feet beam.*

In the coasting trade steamers were at first only employed on regular routes where there was the certainty of a cargo. Steamers cost far more than a sailing ship to buy and maintain, and quick turnround times and constant employment were essential. By the 1850s there was an elaborate network of steamer services linking all the main ports, carrying passengers, cattle and general cargoes. On the cross-channel services there was intense competition between the rival ports and services, and the passenger steamers, elaborately furnished and decorated, took on the appearance of miniature Atlantic liners. The paddle steamers survived on

27. *The Isle of Man Steam Packet Co. had some of the finest and fastest paddle steamers on the west coast; in this picture their 'Queen Victoria' is taking on coal from two flats while at anchor in the river Mersey. Note the miles of docks in the background with the tall masts of deep-sea sailing ships.*

28. *Ritsons' shipyard, Maryport; this busy yard was sited on the river Ellen at the head of the harbour. Vessels built on the main berth had to be launched broadside. In this photograph it is the three-masted barque 'Southerfield' ready for launching in 1881. Ritsons also owned her, until she caught fire off Cape Horn in 1888. Just astern, the wooden paddle tug 'Rambler' is visible.*

29. *Morecambe Bay was harvested for shellfish as well as shrimps. These sturdy clinker-built boats with their standing lugsails sailed out to the mussel beds where the mussels were gathered with long rakes. One of these rakes is just visible lying in the stern thwart of the nearest boat. The horses and carts are a reminder that they were another method of shrimp trawling at low tide in the bay. A nobby can be seen setting sail in the background. The date is about 1890.*

many routes, especially for excursions, because of their excellent manoeuvring characteristics. Some of the later paddlers such as the Isle of Man's *Queen Victoria* had speeds in excess of twenty knots. In the first decade of the twentieth century the first steam-turbine propelled ships were cross-channel steamers.

The transition from sail to steam in the coastal bulk carrying trades was very gradual. An early example of the use of steamers was the fleet of Weaver 'steam packets' which began moving salt cargoes to Liverpool in the 1860s. They had what was to become a standard coaster layout of one long hold amidships, bridge and engines aft, plus a derrick and steam winch. The 1890s saw the building of an increasing number of steam coasters. Large fleets were based on the big ports such as Liverpool, Bristol and Cardiff, and increasingly the shipowners of the small ports turned to steam as well, when they could obtain a regular and profitable trade for them. For example, the Coppack family of Connah's Quay

30. *Boarding the ferries at Liverpool Landing Stage, about 1885. The first Mersey steam ferry in 1816 was the beginning of a major social change. It made commuting from the pleasant Wirral shore to work in grimy Liverpool possible for thousands of people. By 1885 there was an elaborate network of services carrying millions of people every year. This included special 'luggage boats' for carrying vehicles, such as the 'Oxton', the second boat in the photograph.*

began to buy steamers in the 1890s for their staple Point of Ayr coal trade but kept their schooners for the Buckley brick and tile trade where slow hand loading was essential because of the fragility of the cargo. Also, like many other small shipowners, they were very enterprising in obtaining cargoes for their steamers; they developed a summer trade in fruit and vegetables from the Channel Islands to the south coast ports when there was not so much coal to be carried. They even successfully undertook to deliver a cargo of gold-washing machinery to Kimberley in South Africa.

The years 1901 to 1910 saw not only the first steam-turbine propelled ships but the first motorships as well. Most of the early British ones were coasters. There was also an increasing trend to special-purpose vessels

31. *The gasworks ferrymen break their way through the ice floes of Bristol dock, in the late 1890s. Their boat looks stout enough to withstand the ice.*

32. *Campbells' white-funnelled steamers are the most famous of the Bristol Channel excursion steamers. In summer their paddle steamers linked the industrial area of South Wales with the holiday resorts of Somerset and Devon. This particular steamer with the plume of black smoke is the 'Scotia'. Built in 1880 for Scottish owners, Campbells bought her in 1899 and sold her after only a few years. Her crowded decks show the popularity of the sea excursions with our ancestors.*

33. *Steamers for passengers and general cargo made scheduled voyages between all the major ports. Messrs Bacon and Co. ran an excellent service from Liverpool to Bristol and London, with steamers such as the 'Brunswick' (719 tons), built at Glasgow in 1890 and wrecked in 1900 on the English and Welsh Grounds. She is passing the ketch 'Ann' of Cardiff, built at Bristol in 1843, at the dock entrance of Bristol.*

34. *Along the coast of North Wales there were many open anchorages. Vessels risked being blown on to a rocky shore if the weather suddenly changed. At Porthdynllaen, for example, there was a single quay and a jigger flat can be seen loading there (top left). Other vessels, including a large ketch, a steam coaster and a jigger flat with only the mizzen mast visible, await their turn at a risky looking anchorage, close inshore, together with two fishing cutters.*

35. *The work of wooden shipbuilders of the smaller north-western ports is not so well known as that of the famous builders of Portmadoc or Devon and Cornwall. But firms like Marsh & Nicholson at Glasson Dock built some fine vessels. In 1894, their latest was the schooner 'Falcon' for the Fleetwood Pilots. Here she is alongside the quay at Glasson with all sail set for her photograph, after her fitting out.*

36. *Liverpool pilots on station aboard the last pilot schooner 'George Holt', which was sold out of the service in 1905. The pilot in the tam o'shanter is Charles Webster, pilot to the Branch Line, the man at the tiller Sammy Deakin, Booth Line pilot, and the pilot on the extreme right Bill Pemberton, McIver Line pilot.*

37. The first and last in square sail: the first a single temporary sail hoisted on an Avon barge in a fair wind to help her crew, who would otherwise have had to labour with the two huge sweeps, and the last the three-masted barque 'Kilmeny', launched in 1894, being towed up the river Avon to Bristol. She is in the last phase of development of square-sailed ships — a bulk-carrier, with steel masts and rigging and a 'jubilee' or a 'bald-headed' rig without royal yards for maximum economy.

such as tankers to handle all manner of liquids in bulk from crude oil to molasses and now today 'Guinness' (from Dublin to Runcorn). Roll-on roll-off ships and container ships now handle most of the regular sea traffic and the general coasting trade has steadily declined in the face of competition from road transport. There has also been a similar change in deep-sea vessels; the old triple-expansion engined tramp steamer that was so common from the late nineteenth century onwards is almost a vessel of the past. The ocean liner even in its cruising guise is fast becoming extinct. Steam vessels apart from steam-turbine ships are now only to be seen on the west coast among the tugs, dredgers, cranes and other service craft. A few steamers have been preserved; for example, the last coal-fired tug on the Mersey, the *Kerne,* is at present being looked after by a group of local enthusiasts, the *Great Britain* is preserved at Bristol in the dock in which she was built, and the Maritime Trust has bought and is restoring the last steam coaster, the *Robin.* So in this age of the diesel engine a few vessels from the past age of steam survive.

Fishing

Once there were rich fishing grounds off the west coast, in the Irish Sea and in the rivers. Even the Mersey once had the migrating salmon swimming up its broad estuary. Inshore there were shallow waters for shrimps and shellfish like Morecambe Bay, beds of oysters off the Mumbles and, further out, in Cardigan Bay a fine ground for catching turbot, sole, brill and ray, and between the Isle of Man and Liverpool Bay sole, cod, plaice, roker and haddock could be trawled in very profitable quantities. There was also the summer fishery based on Dyfed and the Isle of Man, when large fleets of visiting boats arrived from Devon and Cornwall to share the rich harvest.

During the nineteenth century these grounds were exploited on an increasing scale, first in sailing boats and then from the 1880s by steam trawlers. Fleetwood and Milford Haven became the two most important fishing ports. Both had been optimistically started to exploit the cross-channel passenger traffic and to compete with existing ports for the ocean-going steamship business, and both found their commercial salvation in fishing. The original Fleetwood boats were of about 30 to 40 tons and about 48 feet long on the keel, manned by a crew of five. Similar boats were based on Liverpool, owned and manned by the fishermen of Hoylake, and at Ramsey and Douglas in the Isle of Man. Steam trawling was first tried out on the east coast in 1877 with converted paddle tugs. These improvised trawlers were an immediate success. They brought home bigger catches in better condition. They were no longer dependent on wind and tide. Trawlers specially designed for the job began to be built in increasing numbers, and large fleets came to work from Milford and Fleetwood. There was also a small fleet of no more than twenty steam trawlers started at Liverpool in 1894.

The other important fishing centre was the Isle of Man. The main fishing harbours were Peel, Port Erin and Port St Mary in the south and

38. *Once, the small ports of the west coast were an essential part of the national transport system. Where the railways did not run or where cargoes on offer were small, bulk carriage had to be by water. The sailing schooner and later small steam coaster provided the essential link with the deep-sea ports and this is a typical example: a Welsh 'puffer' loading local grain at Carmarthen in the 1890s, with a two-masted topsail schooner moored further along the quay.*

39. (Right) *HMS 'Thunderer' in the Mersey on a courtesy visit in the mid 1890s. She was completed at Pembroke Dock in 1877 and was a revolutionary design in her day. The old full-sail plan which the Navy had insisted on was completely abandoned and her heavy armament was concentrated into two main turrets.*

west of the island. The original Isle of Man fishing boats were cutter-rigged. Some added a mizzen lugsail in the mid nineteenth century. By the 1870s the local builders began to build copies of the Cornish luggers which worked from the island in the fishing season in large numbers. They were known as 'nickies'. They were extremely fine sea boats, capable of making the stormy passage round the north of Scotland for the Shetland herring-fishing season. A further development of these Isle of Man boats resulted in the 'nobby' with a modified sail plan of standing lugsail on the foremast instead of a dipping one and a bowsprit. At their zenith in the late 1880s there were over 334 of these large fishing vessels owned on the island. The twentieth century saw a rapid decline and after the First World War there were no more than about thirty first-class

40. *The 'Ceres' was the Bristol Channel equivalent of the famous Clyde 'puffers'. She was stoutly built of wrought iron at Cork in 1867 and fitted with a robust and reliable set of compound engines. Her gross tonnage was only 76 tons. When she was photographed at Bristol she was owned by R. Burton of Newport.*

vessels registered in the island's fishing ports.

In addition to what the shipping registers call 'first-class fishing vessels', that is vessels over 15 tons, there was an enormous variety of inshore and estuary fishing craft. They included the coracles of the rivers of South Wales, the Severn, the Conway and the Dee, which were principally used for salmon fishing, the flatners of the river Parrett, a larger version of which served as dumb barges, the Mumbles oyster skiffs, the Tenby luggers, the Aberystwyth beach boats, the Dee salmon boats, and the Morecambe nobbies. The last were by far the most popular type and were used from the Solway Firth as far south as Cardigan Bay. Although there were many variations in detail between the various builders of this type, they were yacht-like cutters of about 30 to 40 feet in overall length. Their lines became more and more extreme, and by the

41. *Ketch 'Jonadab' under full sail in the Bristol Channel. Fair-weather days like this were one of the few compensations in the arduous, back-breaking business of making a living in coastal sail. The 'Jonadab' was built at Newport, Gwent, in 1848 and rebuilt at Saul near Gloucester in 1895. She had a gross tonnage of 68 tons and was owned by William James of Saul when this picture was taken about 1890.*

1890s the original straight stem and square transom had given way to a cut-away stem, rockered keel — often with external ballast — a very hollow, almost V-shaped midships section and a pretty counter stern. They usually carried a big sail area of jib, foresail, mainsail and jackyard topsail. They could be very wet boats in a sea, and the crew worked from a cockpit abaft the mast with high combings. A 20 to 25-foot beam trawl was carried. Shrimps were their main catch and many boats carried a shrimp copper in the cockpit for boiling them before they reached the market. Nobbies were built at Conway, Fleetwood, Barrow, Millom and Arnside. The Crosfields of Arnside were reputed to build the best and fastest boats. They continued building until about 1937. Many nobbies still survive in motorised form or as pleasure yachts, and one at least has been preserved for posterity at Merseyside Maritime Museum.

42. *The number of sailing flats rapidly declined after 1900, and one of their last strongholds was the bunkering of ships at anchor in the Mersey. This photograph shows the old square-sterned flat 'Elizabeth' being loaded with bunker coal at Wellington Dock high-level coaling stage, Liverpool, in 1894.*

Safe navigation and lifesaving

The west coast holds many dangers for ships, and wrecks have been tragically common in the past. The report of the Royal Commission on Unseaworthy Ships of 1873 contains stark evidence of how bad things were in the nineteenth century: in 1862, at a time when facilities for safe navigation and lifesaving were improving, 333 vessels were wrecked or went missing, with the loss of 161 lives, in the coasting trade alone. This figure was for the entire British Isles, but within the total a good number of those poor vessels came to grief on the west coast. The approaches of the big ports show a high concentration of wrecks; the rocky coast of Anglesey claimed many ships inward bound for Liverpool, and the English and Welsh Grounds of the Bristol Channel are littered with wrecks. Some of the vessels in the photographs, such as the steamers *Brunswick* and *The Collier,* were lost there.

During the nineteenth century there was an increasing effort to mark all navigational hazards with buoys, lighthouses or lightships, to provide pilotage services and a rescue service for vessels in distress. These services had existed before but their coverage was uneven and often depended on local voluntary efforts. The work of marking the sea lanes was greatly extended by Trinity House at a national level and by new port authorities such as the Mersey Docks and Harbour Board (created in 1858) at a local level. There were also many technical improvements in the design of sea marks and sea-to-shore communications: for example, the introduction of illuminated buoys and the electric telegraph in the 1850s. The steam engine was a powerful new weapon for the conservancy authorities in their constant fight against silting and shifting channels; steam dredgers and hopper barges were vital to the maintenance of Liverpool's deep-water approach channel in the late nineteenth century when the size of ships was rapidly increasing. Pilot boats were improved and fine seaworthy boats such as the Bristol Channel pilot cutters were developed and built in increasing numbers to cope with the growing demand for their services as the nineteenth century went on. Finally, in the 1890s, steam pilot boats began to make their appearance.

The first national lifeboat service was started in 1824. After great initial enthusiasm and the establishment of a few lifeboat stations such as Barmouth in 1828, the Institution was not very active until it was revived in 1852 with a grand competition to design a self-righting lifeboat. New lifeboat stations were founded in large numbers all along the west coast. This was essential because of the limited range and endurance of sail and pulling boats: there were seven stations to cover Liverpool Bay, where today there is one. Despite the terrible dangers, the brave and hardy crews of these small boats saved many lives. In 1891 the first powered lifeboat on the west coast was put on station at Holyhead — the steamer *Duke of Northumberland*. The twentieth century has seen the general introduction of powered lifeboats (petrol- or diesel-engined rather than steam), and as a result many of the old lifeboat stations have been closed, although some have been revived as inshore rescue stations with fast inflatable boats to rescue holidaymakers in distress. The courageous tradition of the mainly volunteer lifeboat service continues.

43. (Top right) *Sailing trawlers and the paddle tug 'Privateer' (built 1883) off Tenby in the 1890s. Tenby was an important fishing port with its own fleet and many visiting boats, especially from Brixham. The 'Privateer', with her canvas awning, has been turned into a pleasure steamer for the summer to give trips to Tenby's growing number of seaside holidaymakers.*

44. (Bottom right) *A well-loaded flat under sail off the Pier Head, Liverpool, about 1897, the captain at the long tiller, the mate at the mainsheet. Flats were very slow at coming about when fully loaded. Note the massive gear with which she is rigged, including a gaff for discharging cargo stowed alongside the main hatch. They provided plenty of work for the crew of two, but they paid better wages than many shore jobs. In the fine weather the crew have taken off their traditional blue 'guernseys' and are working in their shirt sleeves.*

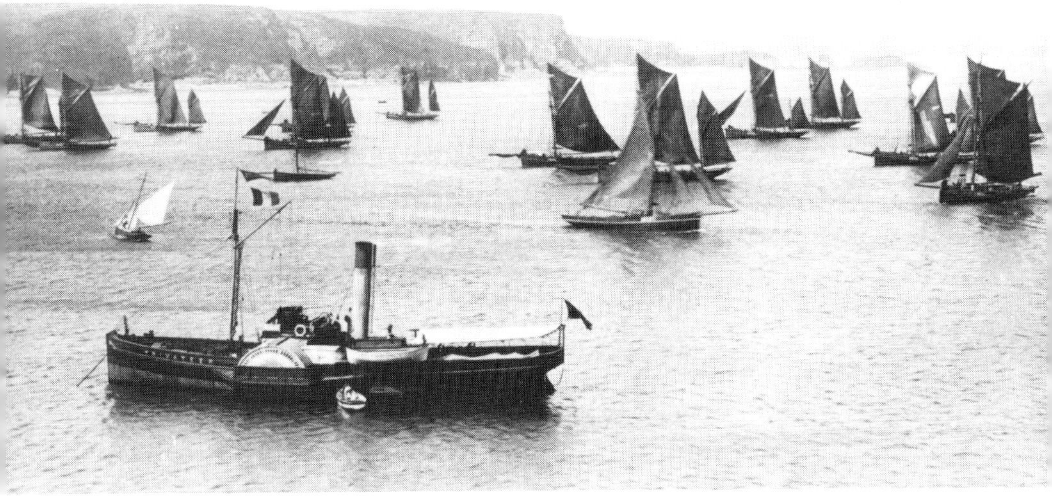

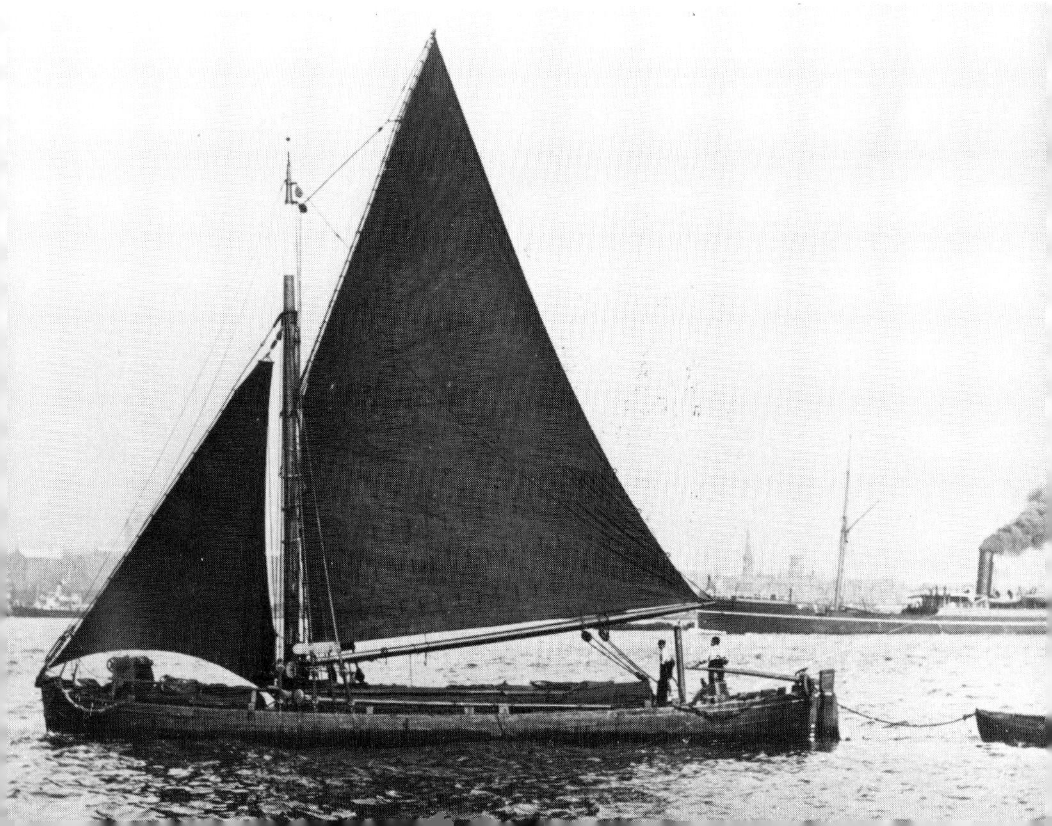

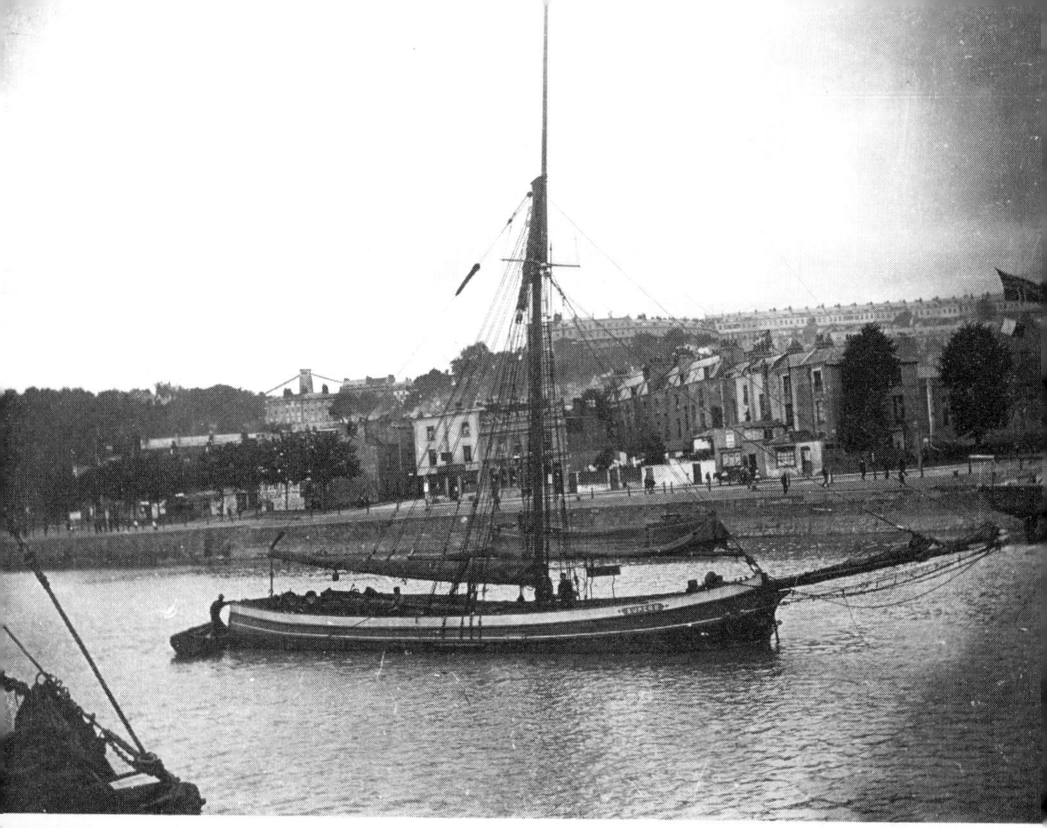

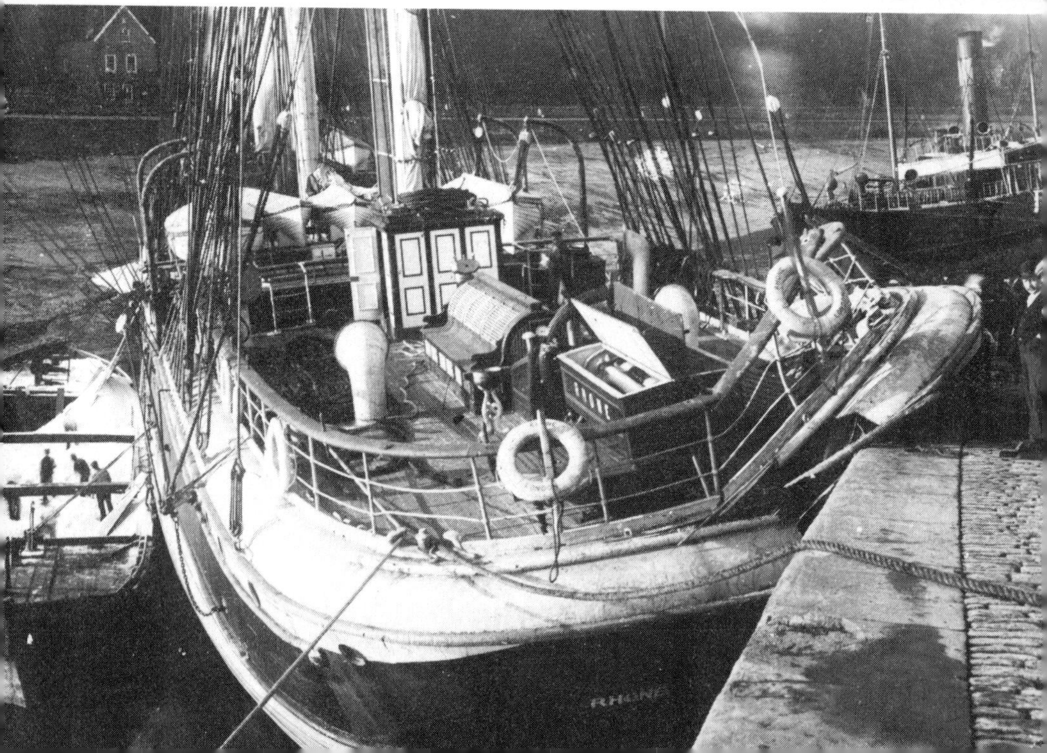
RHONE

47. (Above) *A Hoylake trawler, bound for Liverpool, about 1910. A week's grind of trawling, hauling, sorting and gutting fish is over and the total crew of five relax. The beam trawl is stowed on the starboard side; the thick trawl warp snakes past the pump trunk, and the winch aft known as 'a dandy wink' was used for hauling up the after end of the trawl beam. Note the special baskets, part wicker, part oak lath, for carrying the fish.*

45. (Top left) *The 'Superb' was a trow built up river at Bowers yard, Shrewsbury, in 1826. Her rig with long bowsprit and top mast suggests that at the time of this photograph in the 1890s her work was in the lower Severn and Bristol Channel. She is lying in the Cumberland basin, Bristol, against a background of the fine Georgian terraces of Clifton.*

46. (Bottom left) *The rise and fall of the tide in the river Avon is one of the highest in the country and it was not surprising that occasionally vessels were stranded on the mud. This picture shows the Nourse Line's coolie ship 'Rhone' just off the Bristol locks in January 1896. Apparently the tugs failed to check her in the surging tide and her stern crashed into the dock wall. Her cargo is being discharged by hand into a lighter. This picture gives a good view of the stoutly built furnishings of a sailing ship's poop. In particular, notice the binnacle with the dolphin pedestal.*

48. *Ready to leave, a British three-masted barque is warped through the Canning half-tide dock entrance, Liverpool. This was the place for many a drunken sailor's 'pier-head jump'. Capped and bowlered dockers look on, while the authority of the dock board is represented in the dignified figure of the dockmaster.*

49. *'The Collier' was one of the pioneers of the engines-aft arrangement which became almost standard for coastal steamers. She was built in 1849 at Glasgow and in 1890 she was bought by Pockett's Bristol Channel Packet Co. and steamed into the Avon just as in this photograph many times before she was wrecked in 1914.*

50. *The big four-masted barque 'Donna Francesca' leaves Barry under tow, certainly carrying a cargo of coal or patent fuel and probably bound for some obscure port on the west coast of South America. The last British sailing ships only made profits by systematic parsimony and serving outlandish ports and trades where it would not be economic to send a steamer. The 'Donna Francesca' was one of Russells' noted barques, launched at Greenock in 1892.*

51. *The skipper of the ketch 'Windward' cons his charge to her berth in Canning Dock, Liverpool, under a partially lowered fore staysail. Manoeuvring sailing craft in crowded docks called for fine judgement. The mainsail of the 'Windward' has just been lowered and she has just enough way on her to run gently alongside the two cargo-carrying cutters. The nearer of the two dries out her patched square topsail. She is also fitted with long yard for another square sail; this yard and her long-running bowsprit gave her a sail plan similar to the eighteenth-century revenue cutters. The other cutter has almost completed unloading her cargo of stone. The domed building in the background was the Liverpool Customs House.*

52. *Topsail schooner 'Oak' was built for the Liverpool Dock Trustees in 1836 for carrying granite from their quarries in Kirkcudbrightshire for the building of new docks. This stoutly built vessel carried on this work until 1904. Note the large amount of square sail she carries on her foremast.*

53. *Schooners at Runcorn about 1900; Runcorn, at the head of the Mersey estuary, was an important port for coastal schooners. In particular, they carried large quantities of china clay from Cornwall to Runcorn for transhipment on to the canal system for the Staffordshire potteries. Many schooners were owned and built locally, but the only one that can be identified in this crowded dock is the 'Tregunnel' of Padstow. She, along with the other schooners on the left, have discharged their china clay and are waiting to load coal.*

54. *The smack 'Idris' discharges a cargo of stone on West Kirby beach. She was built at Beaumaris in 1898 and registered as a mere 17 tons. She looks more like a fishing vessel than a cargo carrier, but on the evidence of the stone alongside her she must have carried cargo and as such she was among the last of hundreds of small sloops built on the Welsh coast in the nineteenth century for ferrying freights to creeks and beaches now lost to commerce.*

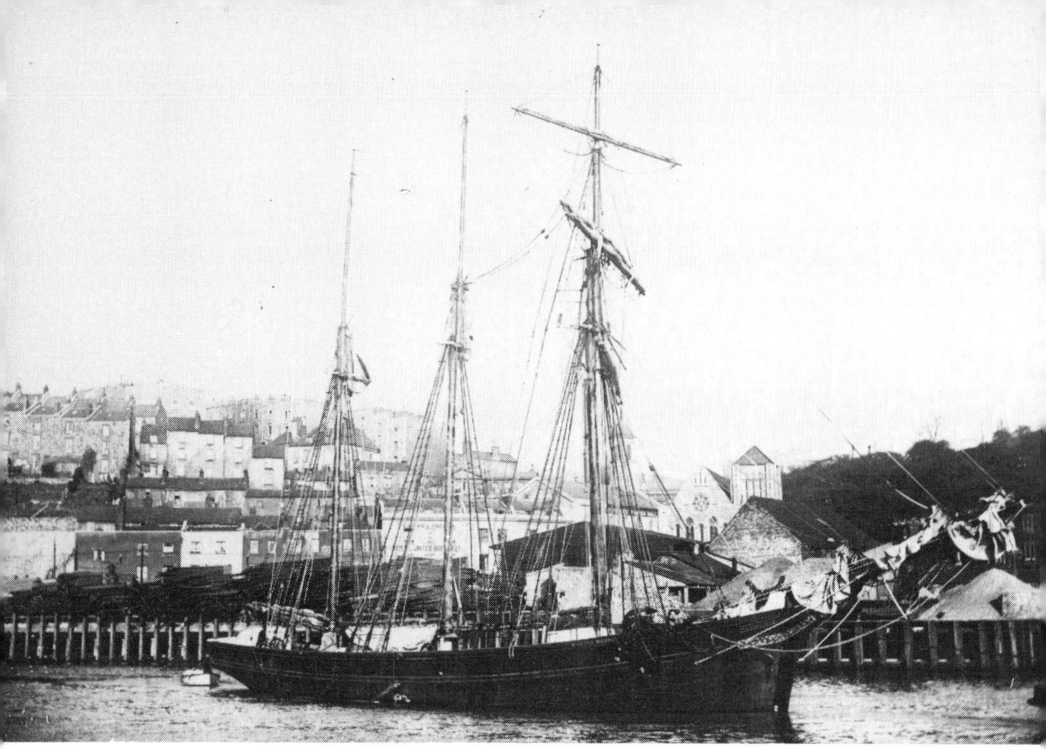

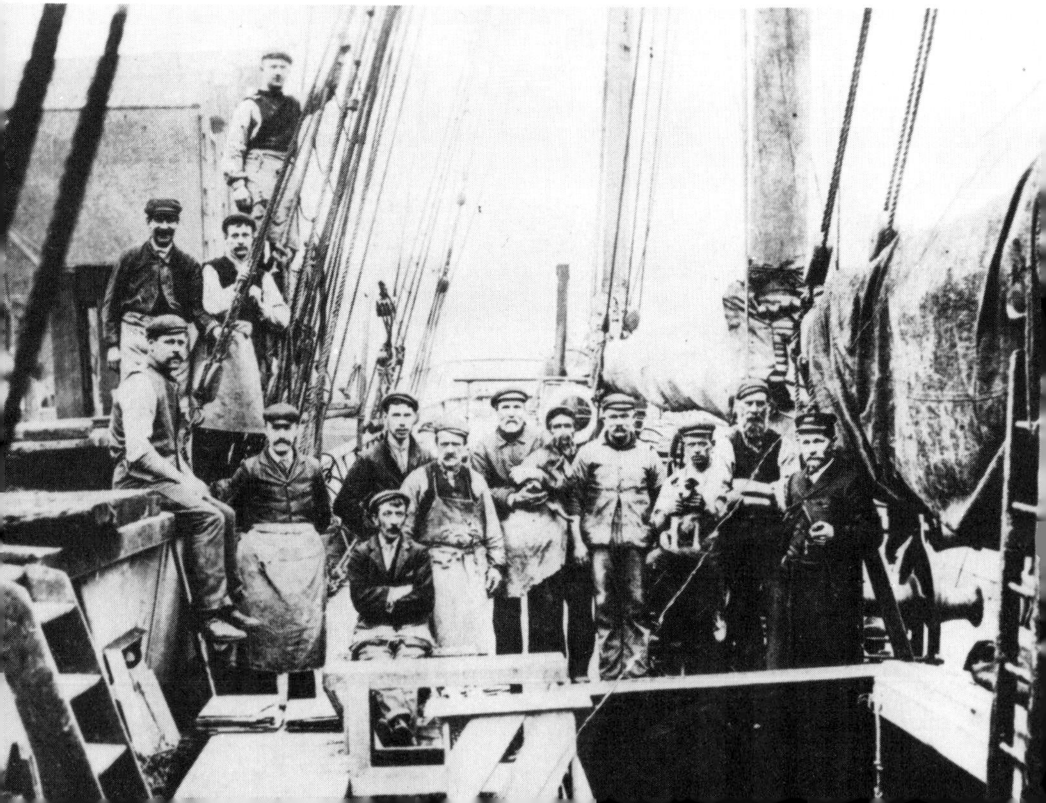

57. (Above) *A Bristol Channel pilot cutter outward bound. These fine sea boats sailed far out beyond the mouth of the Bristol Channel in their quest for incoming ships. They were among the last pilot boats to work under sail and a number have survived as yachts, including the 'Kindly Light' which is to be preserved at Cardiff.*

55. (Top left) *The topsail schooner 'M. Lloyd Morris' passes Brandon Wharf, Bristol, in the early 1900s. Built in 1899 by David Jones of Portmadoc and owned by David Morris of Caernarvon, she has the bold sheer and lofty sail plan which were two hallmarks of the Portmadoc-built ships.*

56. (Bottom left) *Captain Davies (extreme right), his crew and dock labourers take time from unloading slates at Glasson Dock from the schooner 'Mary B. Mitchell' to have their photograph taken. Apart from the captain in his shore-going best suit, their dress and facial expressions reflect the sweat and grime of working in the coastal trade. Even the gear of a coasting schooner was very heavy for the average crew of about four or five.*

58. *Salvage steamer 'Ranger' in the Albert Dock, Liverpool, about 1910. This dock (opened in 1845) was intended to provide secure storage for valuable goods in its imposing range of quayside warehouses. By about 1900 the dock was becoming too small for ocean-going vessels to discharge or load and it became the berth for coasters, barges and service vessels, such as the 'Ranger'. She was an interesting ship for she was originally built as a composite gunboat in 1881. In 1892 she was turned into a salvage vessel by the Liverpool and Glasgow Salvage Association and carried out many successful salvage operations, including seven hundred in the Second World War. She was only scrapped in 1954. Her companion ship, the 'Linnet', lies alongside her and in the background are a trawler, a steam coaster and the dock board's tender 'Vigilant'.*

59. (Right) *Photographs of ships in gales are rare for technical reasons, but the results of a savage gale are often depicted. The Holyhead cattle steamer 'Slieve Gallion', caught in the great gale of 1908, sustained much damage to her bridge, lifeboats and ventilators. Such is the power of the sea.*

60. (Below) *Pilots usually transferred to and from the ships they were guiding by a boarding punt. Occasionally the cutter might run alongside and pick him up, and here Cardiff cutter No. 5 is running close to the outward-bound oil tanker 'Narrangansett' in the early 1900s. It certainly looks a risky operation.*

61. (Above) *The beautiful underwater lines of the barquentine 'May Cory' are revealed at low tide as she lies on the grid-iron at the entrance to Bristol docks. She is a really excellent example of the small British ocean-going sailing ship. She and her sisters were developed for such work as the salt-fish trade from Newfoundland to the Mediterranean. She was built at Bideford in 1875. Note that her hull is sheathed with copper or yellow metal.*

63. (Right) *Lundy Island was one of the navigational hazards of the Bristol Channel. On 30th May 1906 the battleship HMS 'Montagu' ran aground in thick fog on the Shutters, a ledge of rock running out from the island. Despite many salvage attempts, the 'Montagu' could not be prised from the rocks and this almost new battleship became a total wreck.*

62. (Above) *On 12th October 1900 the Norwegian steamer 'Veritas' ran amok in the Mersey. She had been towed in with a damaged engine. While at anchor she was hit by the liner 'Devonian' and careered out of control up the river, chased by two tugs. After capsizing, she was finally swept between the Landing Stage and shore and carried away two of its booms. This photograph shows the dock board's salvage team removing the wreck the next day. The paddle steamer at the stage is the dock board tender 'Vigilant'.*

64. (Above) *Old wooden warships were often put to good use as training ships and reformatories, etc. One of the less well-known was HMS 'Clio', stationed at Bangor. She was built as a 22-gun corvette at Sheerness, a sister ship of the famous 'Challenger'. She was lent to a North Wales society for training boys for a career at sea in 1877 and served in the Menai Straits until she was scrapped in 1920.*

66. (Right) *In the early nineteenth century Holyhead became a flourishing post-office packet port for Ireland. It was one of the first to run a regular cross-channel steamer service. By the time of this photograph of the 'Rathmore' (built in 1903), the size and speed of the ships had greatly increased and the tedious, dirty task of refuelling was handled by an automatic loading barge.*

65. (Below) *'La Marguerite' was one of the most popular and well-known excursion steamers both on the east and west coasts. She was built in 1894 for service on the Thames estuary. In 1904 she was transferred to the Liverpool and North Wales Steamship Co. She proved a great success on their Liverpool-Menai Straits services. She also did good work ferrying troops to France in the First World War. She was scrapped in 1926. This photograph shows her in her heyday packed with day trippers bound for North Wales.*

67. (Left) *Jigger flat 'Eustace Carey' posed with all sail set and firmly moored to the towpath, after her launch from Clare and Ridgeway's yard at Sankey Bridges, near Warrington, in 1905. She was one of the last sailing flats built and was designed for trading coastwise and in particular for carrying chemicals to and from her owner's works at Fleetwood. 'Jigger' or ketch-rigged flats were built in increasng numbers at the end of the nineteenth century. They tended to be larger than the sloop-rigged flats, with a finer entry and ran aft. The 'Eustace Carey' survived afloat until 1965, though latterly without sails. Only her burnt-out hulk is now visible on Widnes Marshes. But Merseyside Maritime Museum has a fine scale model of her in full sail just like this photograph.*

68. (Below) *A square-sterned Mersey flat shoots past the stern of a tug out of Canning half-tide dock, Liverpool. Her mainsail is reefed and two hands are preparing to set her foresail. The arrangement of a flat's rig is clearly visible: the heavy mast is supported by three pairs of shrouds, with an iron rod as a forestry. The wire and chain peak and throat halliards and the topping lifts are all fitted with double purchases and are fed to hand winches at the foot of the mast to ease some of the labour for the small crew. Note also the rib-breaking size of the tiller. This flat is probably on a coastal passage for she carries a crew of four instead of the usual two for river work.*

69. (Above) *Rebuilding Sandon dock, Liverpool, in 1906. The Mersey Docks and Harbour Board owned a small fleet of flats for dock building and maintenance. Here, the Sandon graving docks are being filled in to be replaced by new cargo berths for the increasing trade of the port. The sailing flat 'Chester' is waiting for the steam crane to discharge her cargo of stone. The similarity of her hull form to that of the Humber keel is very marked. This sturdy vessel of 48 tons was built as long ago as 1828, and the derrick flat 'Milo', moored to the caisson, was built in 1848, which says much for the sound construction of these hard-worked craft.*

71. (Right) *The four-masted barque 'Hougomont' is towed into Maryport by the paddle tug 'Conqueror' after being stranded off Allonby in 1903. She had almost completed a voyage from San Francisco to Liverpool. She was being towed when she broke away from her tug and went ashore. She survived the accident and continued trading until 1932 when she was scrapped after being completely dismasted while on passage to Australia.*

70. (Above) *A crowded scene in the Mersey off New Brighton about 1910, with a bucket dredger, a hopper barge and the famous steam lifeboat 'Queen' passed by the suction dredger 'Coronation' inward bound. Dredging in the approach channels and the river was vital to Liverpool as the size of deep-sea steamers increased. In the foreground lies an early example of a motor launch and the nobby 'Mystery', owned by Frank Hughes of Egremont. Note the length of the shrimp trawl beam stowed on deck and that her running bowsprit has been hove in.*

72. (Above) *Port Talbot, like most of the other ports of South Wales, was built in the early nineteenth century (1837) to handle the ever increasing exports of fine Welsh coal. Coal cargoes continued to attract the last generation of deep-sea sailing ships until the 1920s. Here, in 1908 the British ship 'Oceana' is loading at the coal hoist on the right of the picture and the German ship 'Adolphe' (centre) and the four-masted barque 'Kurt' (left) lie at the mooring buoys in ballast waiting their turn to load. The huge 'Kurt' is still afloat as the museum ship 'Moshulu' in the United States, and in this country she is particularly remembered for her voyages under the Finnish flag in the Australian grain trade in the 1930s.*

73. (Top right) *The big splash, an exciting moment for the spectators as the 'Admiral' plunges into her element from Williamsons' yard, Maryport, in 1905. Broadside launches were practised at shipyards where the water space was too small to launch a ship stern first.*

74. (Bottom right) *SS 'Aranci' and topsail schooner 'Ellen Harrison' at Connah's Quay about 1910. This port on the Dee, now abandoned, once thrived on the export of bricks and tiles from the many brickworks of the Buckley area. Schooners and steam coasters were owned and manned by local men, and the famous firm of Ferguson and Baird built fine schooners, such as the 'Kathleen and May', which has been preserved by the Maritime Trust. The 'Aranci' was bought second-hand by the Coppack family in 1899 for her shallow draft, in order to deliver gold and diamond washing machinery made by a local works to Kimberley, South Africa. Coppack sold her in 1913 but continued to run coasting vessels until the 1960s. The 'Ellen Harrison' (73 tons gross) was managed by the other major shipowners of Connah's Quay, the Vickers family. She was built at Ulverston in 1878.*

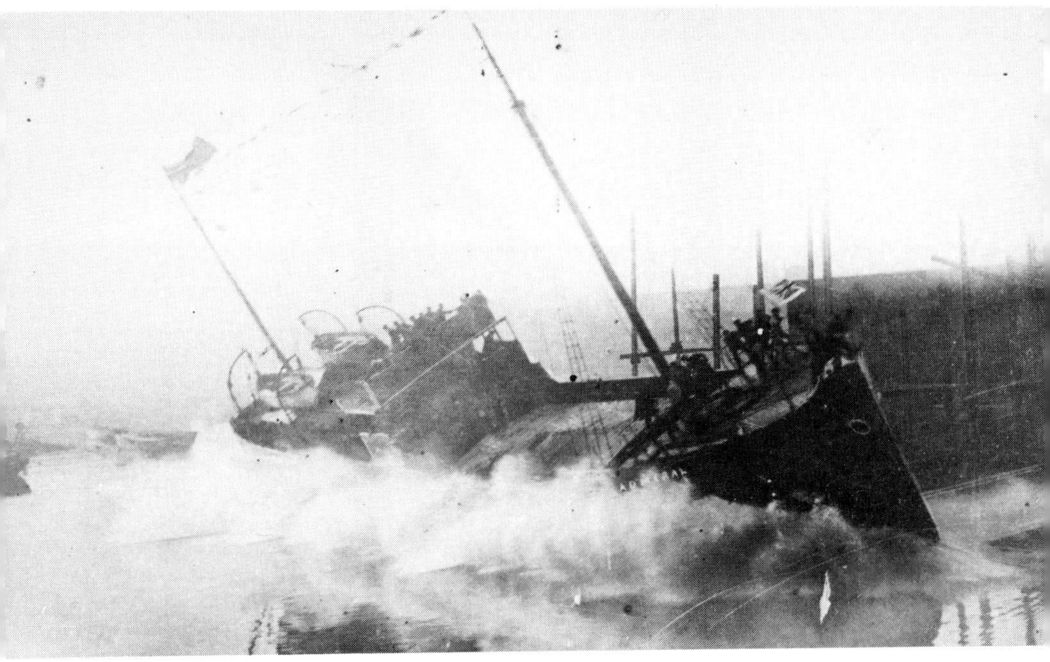

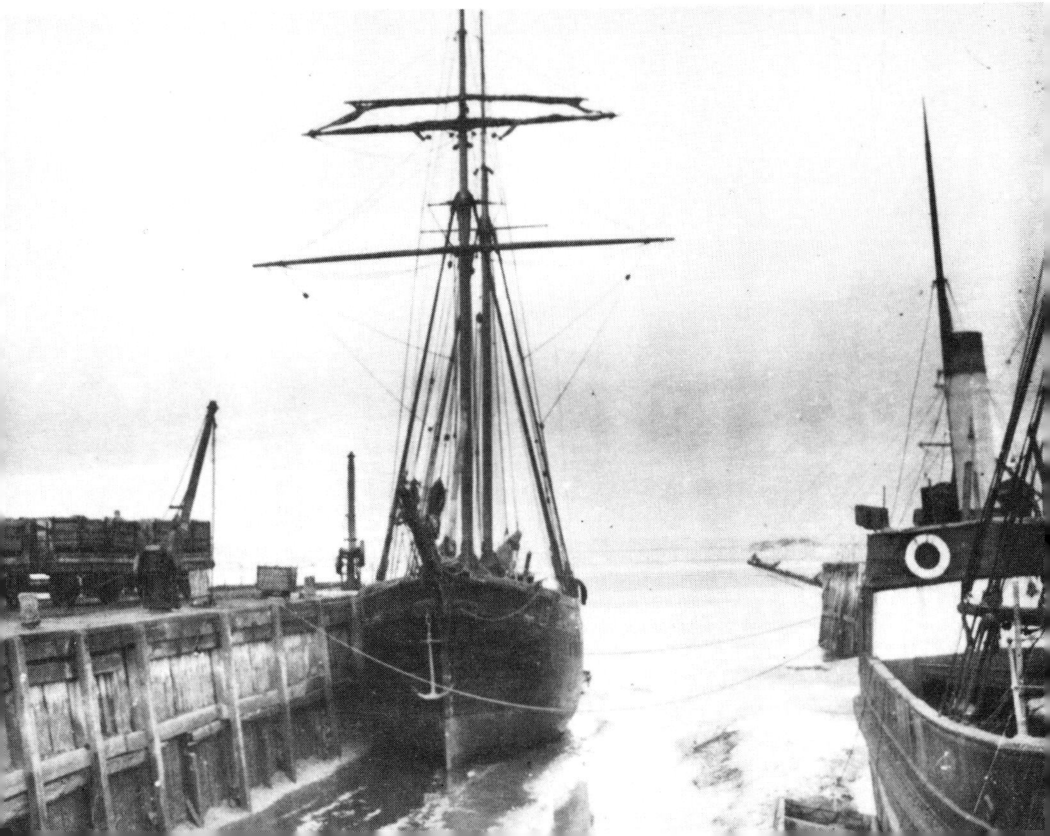

75. *Mersey gigboats in the river, 1904. The gigboats were one of the few examples of sprit-rigged boats on the west coast. They were seaworthy craft and often sailed out as far as Anglesey to meet incoming vessels. Their crews acted as 'hovellers', helping to work ships into dock. By the 1900s the number of gigboats had dwindled with the decline of the deep-sea square-riggers which had been the main customers for their services.*

76. *The Mersey's choppy waters suggest that there is a gale blowing out in Liverpool Bay, and the helmsman on the open bridge of the 276-ton 'Dinorwic', outward bound for North Wales, is in for a wet trip. The White Star liner 'Adriatic' and her tender 'Magnetic' are lying at the Landing Stage.*

77. *Irish-owned coastal sailing vessels were once seen in large numbers on the Mersey. Their staple freight was coal from Garston to Ireland, and the auxiliary schooners of the Tyrells of Arklow perpetuated the traditional run well into the 1950s. This brigantine, the 'Brothers' of Drogheda, is racing up the Mersey under all sail on the flood tide to catch the lock gates at Garston. The date is during the first decade of the twentieth century when brigantines were something of a rarity. She demonstrates the skill of her master-owner Peter Donelly (and indeed many another coastal sailing-ship skipper) when handling his ship under sail alone on the very busy river Mersey. The 'Brothers' (116 tons) was built at Prince Edward Island in 1860 and was one of hundreds of small sailing ships exported from the island's busy shipyards in the mid nineteenth century by the shipowners of the smaller British ports.*

79. (Above) *As the size of ships increased, regular dredging of docks and approach channels became essential in all west coast ports. The grab dredger 'Rhyl' was built in 1911 for the London and North Western Railway for their Garston docks.*

78. (Left) *Crosby Channel buoy 70 is secured on the fore deck of the Mersey Dock and Harbour Board's tender 'Vigilant', 1910. The first buoys were made of oak staves like a barrel and the first iron ones were built in the early nineteenth century. Flashing lights first came into service in the 1850s.*

80. (Below) *Many of the west coast ports have navigational hazards in their approaches and over the last 150 years an elabroate network of lighthouses, buoys and lightships has grown up, mainly under the supervision of Trinity House. One famous seamark was the Bar Lightship off the Mersey, now replaced by a large buoy. The first lightship off the Mersey was a converted galliot in 1813. One of her successors is seen in the photograph, the 'Alarm' of 1912, the most modern lightship of her time.*

81. (Above) *The building of wooden sailing ships for coasting work died out (with a few exceptions) in the first two decades of this century; the ketch 'Emperor' (97 tons) was just such a vessel, built at Chepstow. She was launched in 1906 for a Bristol stone merchant. By 1920 her sails were abandoned and she worked under power. Here she is at Redland wharf, Bristol, with the spire of Saint Mary Redcliff in the background.*

82. (Right) *A 'Barrow flat' topsail schooner, on Tranmere beach about 1910, undergoes temporary repairs at low tide. Two of her crew can be seen hard at work with pitch mops to waterproof her recaulked seams. The caulking was always working loose as the wooden hull was stressed and strained when at sea. Tranmere mud was said to have good leak-stopping qualities too. In the background lie two flats. The term 'Barrow flat' for an Irish Sea schooner was coined by the West Country sailors to denote their special characteristics of a flat bottom and the rudder hung outboard like a flat.*

85. (Above) *The attitudes and expressions of these yachtsmen sum up the pleasures of messing about, repairing boats. In this case, she is an old fishing nobby at Rock Ferry on the Mersey. Some of her gear has been landed on the slip and her running rigging is festooned on deck. Beyond, a dinghy sailor is getting under way, and further out lies the famous old training ship, HMS 'Conway'.*

83. (Top left) *The Mersey in 1914 from the Pier Head, Liverpool, to its entrance at New Brighton. A squadron of cruisers on a courtesy visit is anchored in the centre of the river. Ferries, tugs, freighters and sailing flats are under way and fleets of electric trams are bringing commuters to catch the already packed ferries. The Blackpool-type tower in the background stood at New Brighton until about 1920.*

84. (Bottom left) *The longevity of some coastal sailing vessels was amazing, and the 'Good Intent' of Bridgwater was one of the best examples. A little ketch of only 38 tons, she was built at Plymouth in 1790 and was still trading between Cardiff and Bridgwater with coal in the 1930s, when she was well over one hundred years old.*

86. *Like many another sailing ship caught in an Irish Sea gale, the schooner 'Creek Fisher' dragged her anchors and went ashore. Her crew was saved and she was later salvaged. Many were not so lucky. She was a fine steel schooner built by Rodgers of Carrickfergus for the famous Fishers of Barrow in 1890. In 1916 they had just sold her when she went ashore at Blundellsands.*

87. *The magazine hulk 'Swallow' was stationed off Bromborough on the Mersey for storing high explosive. Four Mersey flats known as 'powder hoys' carried the explosives to the 'Swallow' from Garston and delivered consignments to vessels anchored in 'the powder ground' in Liverpool Bay. They were distinguished by a broad red band and diamonds on the bow. The hoy in the photograph is No. 1 'Bebington' which has been stripped of her sails and motorised.*

88. *Porthgain harbour, packed with four steam coasters loading granite, slates or bricks at the end of the First World War. Today this tiny harbour in Dyfed contains only a few fishing and pleasure boats, and the huge hoppers for granite chippings on the left of the picture, the brickworks, the workers' cottages and the tramway beyond are all abandoned — an industrial archaeologist's paradise. This photograph demonstrates the scale of commercial operations of even such tiny harbours as this in the earlier part of the twentieth century. Three of the ships can be identified: the 'Clwyd' of 289 tons built in 1909 and Liverpool-owned; the 'Volana' of 616 tons, built in 1913 for Rogers & Bright Ltd of Liverpool, and the 'Porthgain', 286 tons, built in 1909, and owned by the United Stone Firms Ltd of Bristol.*

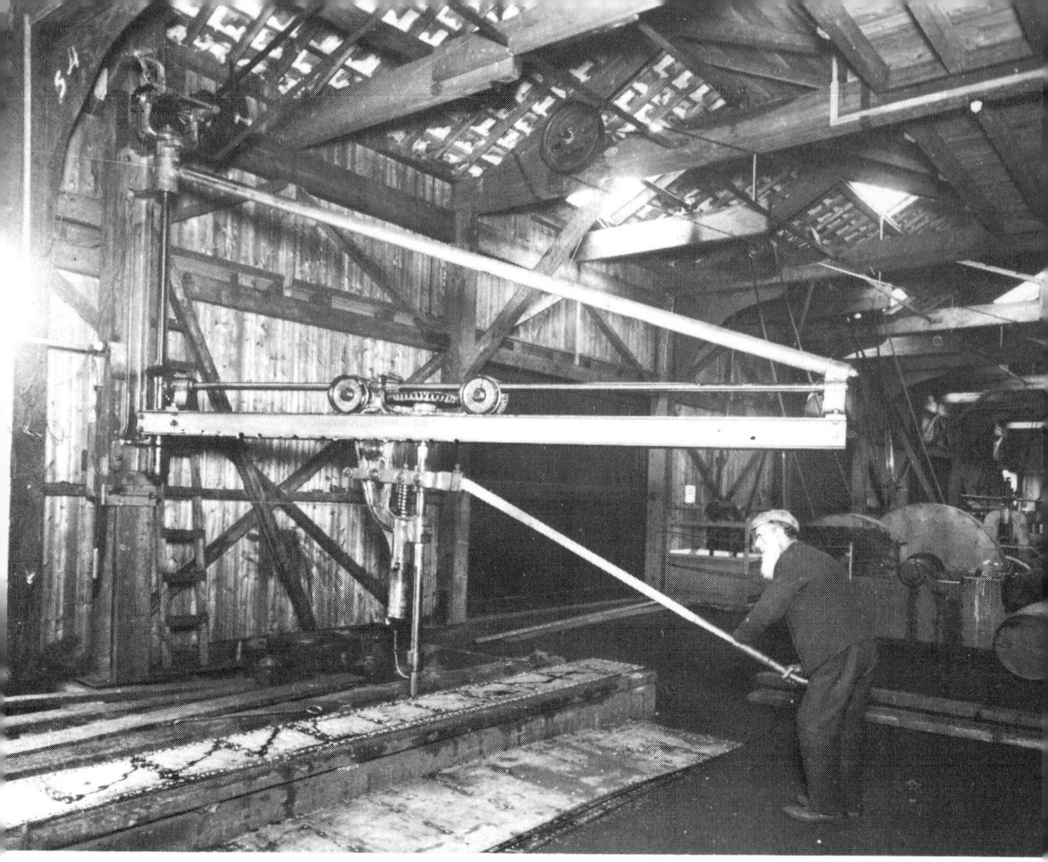

89. (Above) *Isaac Pimblott's shipyard, Northwich, Cheshire, drilling steel plates for the hull of a tug. Pimblotts, like their neighbours, Yarwoods, built all kinds of coastal craft for home waters and for export. In 1906, they moved from their cramped premises in the centre of Northwich to a new site outside the town. The radial drilling machine in the photograph (new in 1906), was still in the shipyard when it closed in 1971.*

91. (Above) *'Johanne', three-masted schooner of Svendborg, Denmark, leaving Douglas, Isle of Man, on 10th August 1925 after discharging a cargo of sawn timber. This was a regular trade for these shapely Scandinavian vessels and in the 1920s as many as four of them at one time could be seen in the Inner Harbour at Douglas.*

90. (Left) *This deceptively ordinary-looking coaster, the 'Fullagar', was in fact a turning point in shipbuilding technique. Launched by Cammell-Laird & Co., Birkenhead, in 1920, she had the first all-welded hull ever built.*

94. (Above) *The stern wheeler is not on some exotic tropical river but the river Weaver, at Northwich in Cheshire. The 'Roxby' was one of hundreds of small craft once exported by the small shipyards of the west coast to all parts of the world. Northwich, for example, had two such yards until the 1960s, Yarwoods and Pimblotts, building excellent barges for the local river and stern wheelers like the 'Roxby', launched in the 1930s for more distant parts.*

92. (Top left) *Morecambe Bay nobbies racing about 1920 at Morecambe Regatta, left to right, 'Celeste', 'Anne' (FD108) and 'Alice Allan'. These yacht-like cutters were developed at the end of the nineteenth century for inshore trawling, especially for shrimps. They worked in large numbers in Morecambe Bay, Southport, the Mersey and North Wales. They were usually about 35 feet long and their fine hull lines, combined with a large sail area, gave the speed necessary to race their perishable catches to market. They were worked by a crew of two and quite a number are motorised and still working as fishing boats.*

93. (Bottom left)*Morecambe Bay can be a dangerous place for small fishing boats. Sudden squalls can transform its shoal waters into a vicious sea very quickly. The local nobbies were built to work in these conditions and this view shows the 'Alice Allan' trawling for shrimps under reefed mainsail and jib in rough weather. Although she is staggering under the drag of the heavy beam trawl, her copper for boiling the catch is alight and smoking.*

95. (Left) *Three-masted schooner 'De Wadden' motors across the dock at Preston in 1934. She is one of the last schooners to trade commercially. Up to the 1960s she often carried coal cargoes from Garston on the Mersey to Irish ports. She is now owned by the Merseyside Maritime Museum.*

96. (Below) *The Fleetwood trawler 'Eddystone' steams past the local Knott End ferry outward bound for the Icelandic fishing grounds. Fleetwood was conceived as a railway and cross-channel port but found its fortune in the 1890s as a base for a large fleet of steam fishing trawlers. It is still a major fishing port, but the steam trawlers have given way to motor vessels.*

97. *The tugmasters' skill in manoeuvring a big ship in or out of dock is put to the test at Liverpool's Sandon dock entrance. A combination of three Alexandra Towing Co. tugs and the tender 'Magnetic' (far left) are in charge of the White Star liner 'Baltic', just arrived from New York in 1925. Tugs were one of a whole range of essential service craft in all the main ports of the west coast.*

98. (Above) *Cardiff was one of the last ports to receive small wooden sailing ships and the Breton schooners, like this pair in Bute Dock, were regular visitors to the port until the Second World War. They usually brought cargoes of pitwood or onions, and loaded coal for the return trip. They were fast vessels and frequently made the passage from ports such as Roscoff or Trequier to Cardiff in under four days. Unlike the British schooners, which survived to the 1930s, they retained their square topsails when they were fitted with an auxiliary engine. In 1937 there were some twenty-one of these ships, but by August 1939 the number had been reduced to only thirteen by loss or sales to Scandinavian owners.*

99. (Top right) *The 'J. & M. Garratt' was a typical 'Barrow flat' schooner with the neat round stern and the rudder hung outboard. She was built at Barrow by the famous Ashburner shipyard in 1884 and was owned at Connah's Quay. In 1935 she was docked at Bridgwater, Somerset, where this photograph was taken, and she has lost her square topsails, except for a light fair-weather square sail, and gained two diesel auxiliary engines. The wind might be free but the cost of replacing sails and gear was a heavy drain on the sailing ship's earnings. In the difficult times of the 1930s penny-saving economy was the only way to make any money in schooners, and expensive sails like the topsails were often dispensed with.*

100. (Bottom right) *These two tugs, the 'Furness' and the 'Ramsden', remind us of the origins of their home port. Barrow was founded by the Furness Railway, under the chairmanship of James Ramsden, in the 1840s as port for the local iron-ore trade and cross-channel passenger traffic. Later in the nineteenth century, huge docks were built to attract some of the North Atlantic trade from Liverpool. Although Barrow's hopes of becoming a major port remained unfulfilled, the port became the site of a huge Vickers Armstrong shipbuilding yard. Vickers since 1871 have built many fine ships, including the P & O liner 'Stratheden', launched in 1937 and seen in this photograph in the fitting-out basin at Barrow under tow by the 'Ramsden' and the 'Furness'.*

Bibliography

Bouquet, M. *No gallant ship*. Carter & Hollis. 1959.

Bouquet, M. *West Country sail, 1840-1960*. David & Charles. 1970.

Coppack, Tom. *A lifetime with ships*. Stephenson. 1973.

Duckworth, C. L. D. and Langmuir, G. E. *West coast steamers*. Stephenson. 1966.

Eames, A. *Ships and seamen of Anglesey*. Anglesey Antiquarian Society. 1973.

Farr, G. E. *Chepstow ships*. The Chepstow Society. 1954.

Farr, G. E. *West Country steamers*. Stephenson. 1967.

Farr, G. E. *Wreck and rescue in the Bristol Channel*. Bradford Barton. 1966.

Greenhill, Basil. *The merchant schooners*. David & Charles. 1968.

Hughes, E. and Eames, A. *Porthmadog ships*. Gwynedd Archives Service. 1975.

March, E. J. *Inshore craft of Britain* (volume 2). David & Charles. 1970.

March, E. J. *Sailing drifters*. David & Charles. 1969.

March, E. J. *Sailing trawlers*. David & Charles. 1970.

Stammers, M. K. *Historic ships*. Shire. 1987.

Stammers, M. K. *Tugs and towage*. Shire. 1989.

Tomlinson, E. W. Paget. *Mersey and Weaver flats*. Robert Wilson. 1973.

Wall, Robert. *Bristol Channel pleasure steamers*. David & Charles. 1973.

White, E. W. *British fishing boats and coastal craft*. HMSO. 1950.

PHOTOGRAPHIC ACKNOWLEDGEMENTS

Photographs are acknowledged as follows: Dr Dennis Chapman, 5, 47, 67, 70, 82, 85, 87; D. B. Cochrane, 95; R. M. Cookson, 51; G. E. Farr, 99; A. A. Hurst, 57, 72, 84; K. Lewis, title page; Dr Lewis Lloyd, 2; N. Morrison, 36; D. Sattin, 95; D. E. Smith, 91; M. K. Stammers, 20, 34; D. G. Sythes, 21, 28, 73; Dr Charles Waine, 74; Keith Willacy, 29, 92, 93; M. Wilson, 101; Roger Worsley, 23, 24, 43, 88; Bristol City Museum, 7, 11, 15, 16, 19, 31, 32, 33, 37, 40, 41, 45, 46, 49, 50, 55, 60, 61, 81; Lancashire Libraries, 96; Lancaster Museum, 35, 56; Liverpool District Engineer's Reprographic Section, 1, 44; Merseyside Maritime Museum, 6, 8, 9, 10, 12, 13, 14, 17, 18, 22, 26, 27, 30, 38, 39, 42, 48, 52, 53, 54, 58, 59, 63, 64, 65, 66, 68, 71, 75, 76, 77, 79, 80, 83, 89, 90, 94, 100, page 2, cover; Mersey Docks & Harbour Co., 62, 69, 78, 86, 97; National Maritime Museum (from the Lacock Abbey Collection), 3, 4; Newport Museum and Art Gallery, 25.

Index

Aberystwyth 9, 14, 16, 42
Allonby 9, 65
Amlwch 6
Anglesey 14, 45, 68
Arnside 43
Avon, river 12, 22, 38, 48, 50
Avonmouth 23
Ayr 24
Barmouth 7, 46
Barque 15, 18, 23, 24, 32, 38, 50, 51, 65, 66
Barquentine 10, 58
Barrow flat 73, 85
Barrow-in-Furness 16, 19, 20, 24, 43, 85
Barry 51
Bath 27
Beach boat 9, 42
Beaumaris 53
Bideford 10, 58
Birkenhead 19, 38
Blundellsands 76
Bridgwater 16, 74, 85
Brig 2, 10, 15, 16, 18, 24
Brigantine 9, 15, 19, 21, 69
Bristol 6, 10, 13, 16, 18, 23, 27, 30, 33, 35, 36, 38, 42, 48, 54, 58, 72
Brixham 29, 47
Bromborough 77
Brunel, I. K. 27
Caernarvon 16, 26, 54
Cardiff 13, 22, 33, 54, 57, 74, 84
Carmarthen 40
Castletown 18, 31
Cattle steamer 57
Chepstow 25, 72
Chester 13
Coaster, steam 1, 2, 36, 38, 40, 50, 56, 77, 78
Connah's Quay 6, 14, 16, 19, 24, 33, 67, 85
Conway 42, 43
Coracle 42
Cunard, Samuel 27
Cutter 20, 36, 40, 42, 45, 51, 55, 57, 80
Dee, river 42, 67
Derrick flat 64
Douglas 39, 79
Dredger 11, 14, 38, 45, 65, 71
Drogheda 69
Dublin 27, 38, 88
Dundalk 24
Ellesmere Port 23
Eriska 24
Flat 4, 9, 11, 15, 20, 22, 23, 36, 44, 46, 47, 62, 63, 64, 73, 74
Flatner 42
Fleetwood 24, 39, 43, 62, 82
Full-rigged ship 11, 15, 16

Garston 69, 71, 77, 82
Gigboat 68
Glasgow 27, 36, 50
Glasson Dock 37, 54
Harrington 14
Holt, Alfred 28
Holyhead 27, 46, 57, 61
Hoylake 39, 49
Ilfracombe 22
Jigger flat 23, 36, 62
Jones, Rev. Calvert 7, 8, 14
Ketch 15, 16, 19, 20, 22, 23, 26, 36, 41, 51, 72, 74
Lancaster 13
Lifeboat 6, 28, 46, 65
Lightship 11, 45, 71
Liner 11, 38, 68, 83, 85
Liverpool 2, 5, 6, 8, 10, 11, 13, 16, 17, 20, 25, 27, 33, 34, 36, 39, 44, 47, 49, 50, 51, 56, 59, 60, 63, 64, 65, 74, 83
Llanelli 2
Lugger 42
Lundy Island 59
Lydney 25
Magazine hulk 77
Man, Isle of 5, 6, 18, 27, 29, 31, 33, 39, 40, 88
Maryport 14, 32, 65, 67
Menai Straits 60
Mersey, river 2, 4, 8, 10, 11, 12, 20, 23, 32, 34, 38, 39, 40, 44, 52, 59, 65, 68, 69, 71, 74, 75, 80, 82
Mersey flat 4, 20, 22, 23, 63, 77
Milford Haven 6, 13, 27, 29, 30, 39
Millom 14, 43
Morecambe/Morecambe Bay 33, 39, 42, 80
Motorship 34
Mumbles 39, 42
Naval vessels 11, 41, 59, 60, 74
New Brighton 11, 65, 74
Newport (Gwent) 13, 22, 24, 30, 42, 43
Nicky 29, 31, 40
Nobby 6, 31, 33, 39, 42, 43, 65, 75, 80
Northwich 5, 78, 81
Paddle-steamer 5, 6, 8, 11, 12, 22, 27, 31, 32, 33, 35, 46, 59, 65, 81
Padstow 52
Parrett, river 42
Peel 29, 39
Pembroke Dock 6, 40
Pilot vessels 9, 11, 20, 37, 45, 46, 55, 57
Plymouth 24, 26, 74
Port Erin 39
Porthdynllaen 36
Porthgain 77

Portishead 22, 23
Portmadoc 5, 7, 14, 16, 24, 54
Port St Mary 29, 39
Port Talbot 66
Powder hoy 77
Preston 82
Prince Edward Island 69
Puffer 40, 42
Ramsey 39
Rock Ferry 75
Runcorn 16, 23, 27, 38, 52
St Davids 27
Salmon boat 42
Salvage steamer 56
Saul 43
Saundersfoot 14
Schooner 5, 6, 9, 10, 11, 12, 15, 16, 18, 19, 20, 21, 24, 25, 26, 31, 34, 37, 40, 52, 54, 67, 73, 76, 79, 82, 84, 85
Severn, river 22, 42
Severn trow 20, 22
Sheerness 60
Shrewsbury 48
Silloth 15, 88
Skiff 42
Sloop 15, 20, 22, 53

Smack 20, 25, 26, 53
Snow 7, 15, 18
Southport 6, 80
Square-rigger 6, 15, 18, 68
Stern wheeler 81
Swansea 8, 9, 13, 14, 16
Tenby 14, 22, 29, 42, 46, 47
Tender 56, 59, 68, 70, 83
Topsail schooner 6, 11, 12, 15, 18, 24, 40, 52, 54, 67, 73
Training ship 60, 75
Tramp steamer 38
Tranmere 73
Trawler 6, 29, 30, 39, 46, 49, 56, 82
Trow 6, 11, 15, 20, 22, 48
Tug 8, 11, 12, 14, 29, 32, 38, 46, 65, 74, 83, 85
Ulverston 67
Walters, Samuel 8
Warrington 62
West Kirby 53
Weston Point 23
Wherry 9
Whitehaven 13, 14, 16, 19, 21, 24
Workington 14, 28
Wrecks 6, 45, 59

101. *SS 'Yarrow' steams out of Silloth, 1927. She was a local institution in this small Cumbrian cross-channel port. People invariably turned out to see her arrive or sail. From 1893 until the Second World War she plied her way from Silloth to the Isle of Man and Dublin with general cargo, passengers and cattle. In 1929 the Dublin, Douglas & Silloth SS Co. sold her to Palgrave and Murphy who renamed her 'Assaroe' but retained her on her usual run.*